I0814940

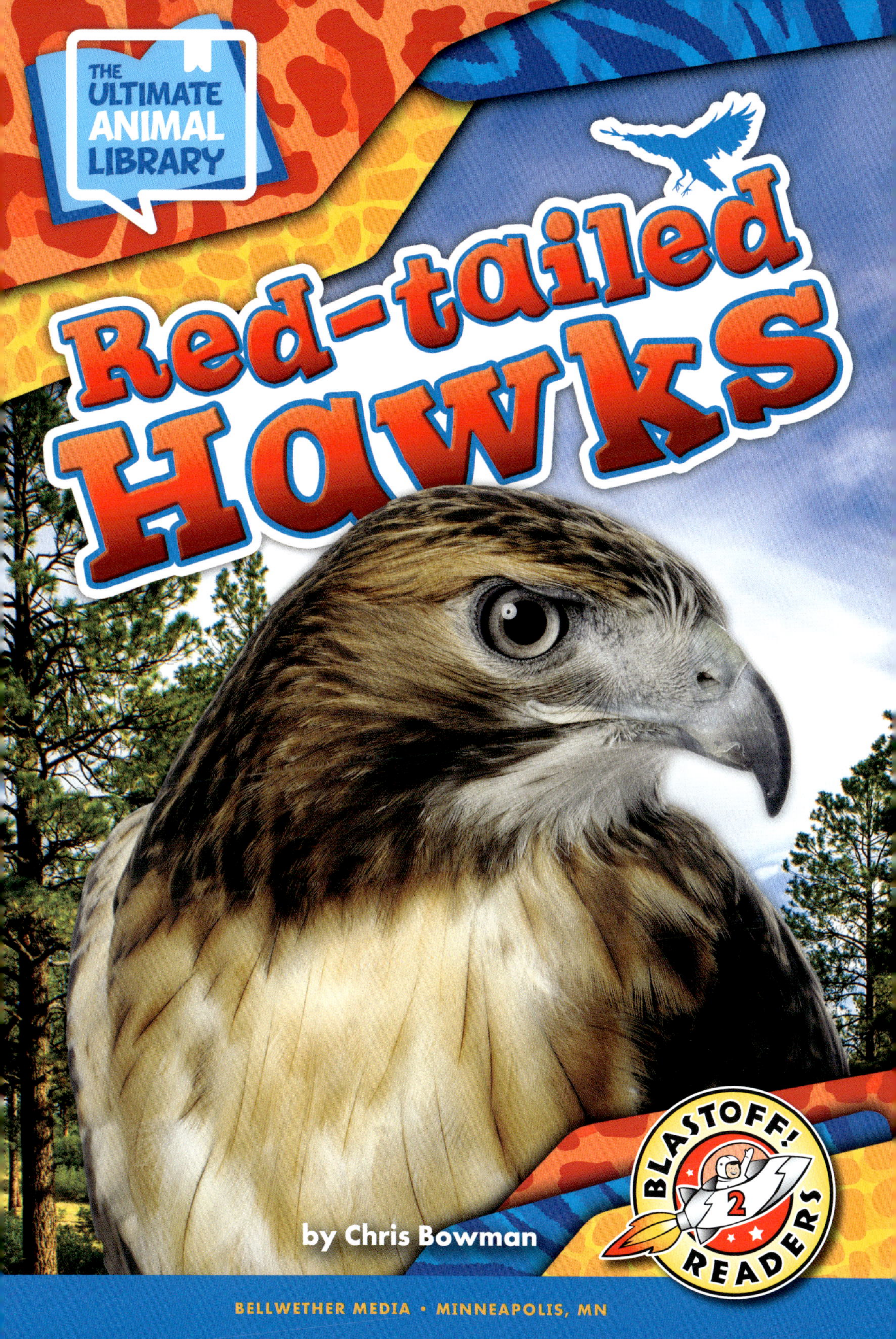
THE ULTIMATE ANIMAL LIBRARY
Red-tailed Hawks
by Chris Bowman
BLASTOFF! 2 READERS
BELLWETHER MEDIA • MINNEAPOLIS, MN

Blastoff! Readers are carefully developed by literacy experts to build reading stamina and move students toward fluency by combining standards-based content with developmentally appropriate text.

LEVELS

Level 1 provides the most support through repetition of high-frequency words, light text, predictable sentence patterns, and strong visual support.

Level 2 offers early readers a bit more challenge through varied sentences, increased text load, and text-supportive special features.

Level 3 advances early-fluent readers toward fluency through increased text load, less reliance on photos, advancing concepts, longer sentences, and more complex special features.

★ Blastoff! Universe

Reading Level

Grade K

Grades 1–3

Grade 4

This edition first published in 2025 by Bellwether Media, Inc.

Library of Congress Cataloging-in-Publication Data

Names: Bowman, Chris, 1990- author.
Title: Red-tailed hawks / by Chris Bowman.
Description: Minneapolis, MN : Bellwether Media, Inc., 2025. | Series: Blastoff! Readers. The ultimate animal library | Includes bibliographical references and index. | Audience: Ages 5-8 | Audience: Grades 2-3 | Summary: "Relevant images match informative text in this introduction to red-tailed hawks. Intended for students in kindergarten through third grade"-- Provided by publisher.
Identifiers: LCCN 2024038370 (print) | LCCN 2024038371 (ebook) | ISBN 9798893042436 (library binding) | ISBN 9798893043402 (ebook)
Subjects: LCSH: Red-tailed hawk--Juvenile literature. | Red-tailed hawk--Life cycles--Juvenile literature.
Classification: LCC QL696.F32 B6677 2025 (print) | LCC QL696.F32 (ebook) | DDC 598.9/44--dc23/eng/20240911
LC record available at https://lccn.loc.gov/2024038370
LC ebook record available at https://lccn.loc.gov/2024038371

Editor: Elizabeth Neuenfeldt Series Designer: Veah Demmin

Printed in the United States of America, North Mankato, MN.

Table of Contents

What Are Red-tailed Hawks?

Red-tailed hawks are **raptors**. They live in North America and Central America. They are named for their red tail feathers!

Red-tailed Hawk Report

These hawks have mostly brown heads and backs. Some feathers look black.

Their chests and bellies are mostly white.

wingspan

Red-tailed hawks have big wings. Their **wingspan** can be over 4 feet (1.2 meters) wide.

They weigh up to 4 pounds (1.8 kilograms). Females are usually larger than males.

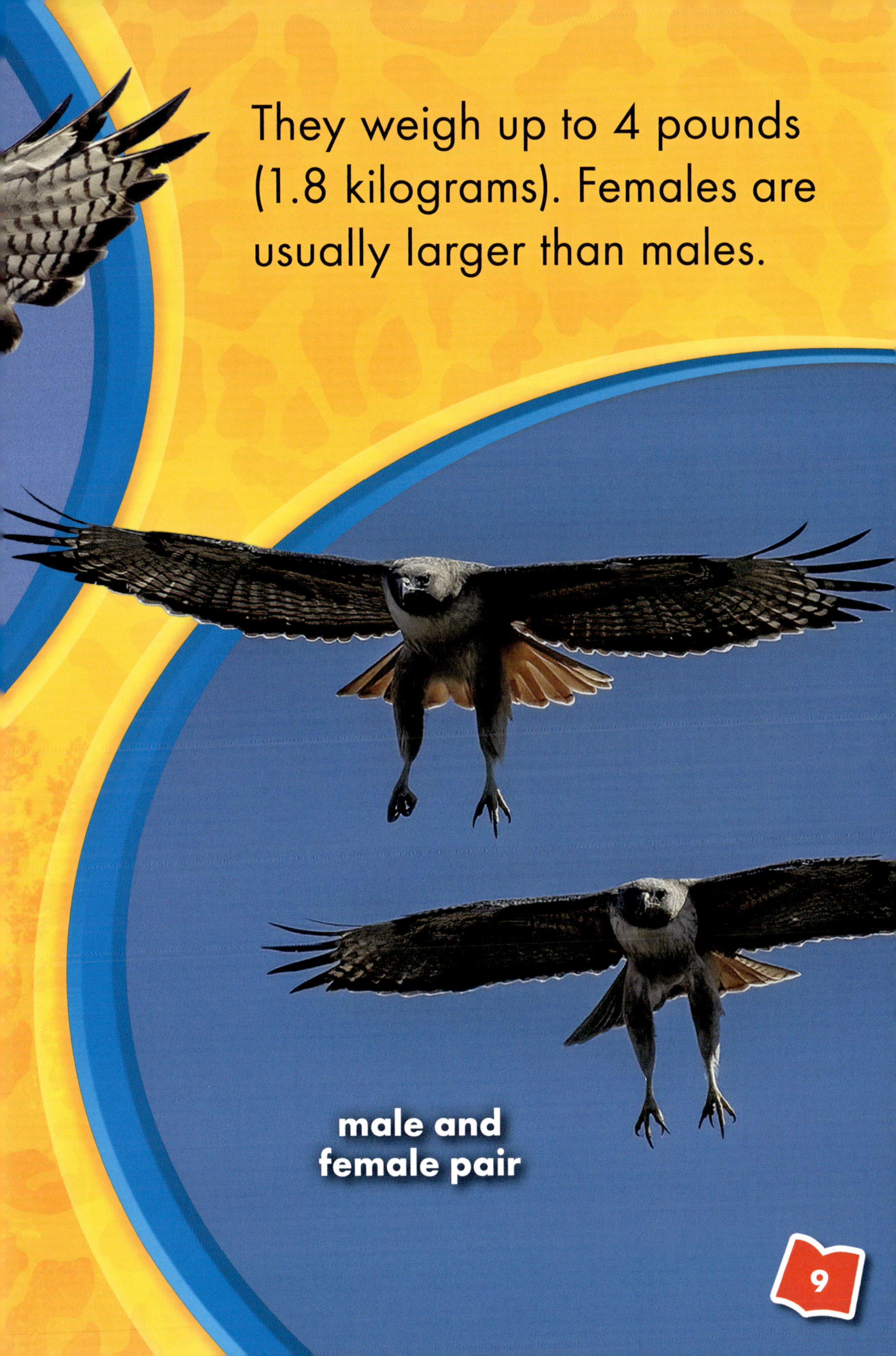

male and female pair

Red-tailed hawks have curved beaks. Their **talons** are sharp.

They use their beaks and talons to tear **prey** apart.

Spot a Red-tailed Hawk
red tail feathers
big wings
curved beak
prey

Sharp-eyed Hunters

Red-tailed hawks are often found near forests and **grasslands**.

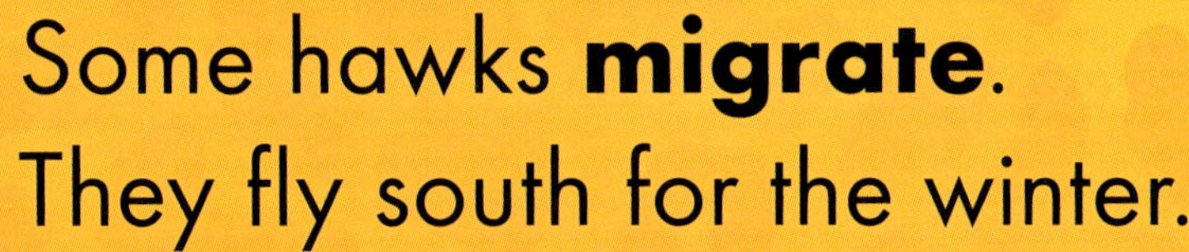

Some hawks **migrate**.
They fly south for the winter.

These hawks often live in pairs. They share and guard a **territory**.

They build nests together. They usually build their nests on treetops.

These hawks have great eyesight.
They find prey from the air
or on a **perch**.

Red-tailed Hawk Food Web

mice

snakes

small birds

They eat mice and rabbits.
Snakes and small birds
also make a quick meal.

Growing Up

Females lay up to five eggs at a time. Both parents keep the eggs warm.

The eggs **hatch** after about four weeks. **Chicks** come out. Both parents raise the chicks.

chicks

fledgling

Fledglings leave the nest after about six weeks. They stay nearby as they get better at flying.

Then they fly off
on their own!

Life of a Red-tailed Hawk

Name of Babies

chicks

Number of Eggs

up to 5

Time Spent in Eggs

about 4 weeks

Life Span

Glossary

chicks—baby red-tailed hawks

fledglings—young birds that have feathers for flight

grasslands—lands covered with grasses and other soft plants with few bushes or trees

hatch—to break open

migrate—to travel from one place to another, often with the seasons

perch—a place where birds sit and rest

prey—animals that are hunted by other animals for food

raptors—large birds that hunt other animals; raptors have excellent eyesight and powerful talons.

talons—the strong, sharp claws of red-tailed hawks and other raptors

territory—the area where an animal lives

wingspan—the distance from the tip of one wing to the tip of the other wing

To Learn More

AT THE LIBRARY

Gish, Melissa. *Hawks.* Mankato, Minn.: Creative Education and Creative Paperbacks, 2024.

Rathburn, Betsy. *Brilliant Birds.* Minneapolis, Minn.: Bellwether Media, 2023.

Scheffer, Janie. *Bald Eagles.* Minneapolis, Minn.: Bellwether Media, 2025.

FACTSURFER

Factsurfer.com gives you a safe, fun way to find more information.

1. Go to www.factsurfer.com.

2. Enter "red-tailed hawks" into the search box and click .

3. Select your book cover to see a list of related content.

Index

The images in this book are reproduced through the courtesy of: Robert Eastman, front cover; Dominic Gentilcore PhD, front cover background, interior background; arsal1, front cover (hawk icon); Le Do, p. 3; Ondrej Prosicky, p. 4; mlorenz, p. 6; Leena Robinson, p. 7; ranchorunner, pp. 8, 23; Channel City Camera Club/ Wikipedia, p. 9; Ronnie Howard, p. 10; Georgi Baird, pp. 10-11; Brent Simon, p. 11; Stanislav Duben, p. 12; Susan Hodgson, p. 13; Casey_Lynn_Photography, p. 14; Jim Lambert, p. 15; Harry Collins Photography, pp. 16-17; Mahi ryan, p. 17 (red-tailed hawk); Martin Pelanek, p. 17 (mice); Lisa Basile Ellwood, p. 17 (snakes); Travis Potter, p. 17 (small birds); Johann Schumacher/ Alamy, p. 18; Breck P. Kent, pp. 18-19; Randy G. Lubischer, p. 20; Thomas O'Neil, p. 21.